From An Idea To Reality
The Entrepreneurs Guide
To Starting A Business

By Markeeta Stokes, Lamika Jenkins

From an Idea To Reality
Text Copyright @ 2017 by Markeeta Stokes

No part of this book may be used or reproduced in an manner whatsoever without written permission except in the case of brief quotations embodied in critical articles and reviews.

Congratulations on taking the Entrepreneurial aka Risk Taker Leap of Faith! This book will walk you through the basics of starting a business and maintaining your sanity throughout the process. Remember if your foundation isn't solid whatever you build on it will crumble.

The one question that you should ask yourself before reading any further. Why am I starting a business? Having a clear idea of the answer to this question will help you throughout your business building process. Every business started out as an idea but was further cultivated to bring forth a viable service and/or product. Having a solid plan and access to knowledge to assist you is critical for your long term success.

Start-up success or failure is all about knowing both how and the why of taking action, and always being clear about which steps to take next.

Chapter 1
Determine Your Foundation Structure

One of the first things you must decide when starting a business is how you want to structure your organization. It's always important to thoroughly research each ownership type and decide which structure is best for your business. The choice will depend solely on your personal situation so make sure you give it great thought. This decision will not only impact how much you pay in taxes for your business, but it will affect the amount of paperwork your business is required to complete, the personal liability you face and your ability to raise capital. So keep these three important components in mind when making your decision.

>   1. **Liability** - Your businesses financial debt or obligations that emerge during the course of its business operations.

2. **Taxation** - The amount of taxes you have to pay the government

3. **Record Keeping** - This is how you collect and maintain all the pertinent information and financial data for your business.

Now lets get into the basic types of business ownerships.

Sole Proprietor - This is also known as a sole trader or a proprietorship which involves a single owner who pays personal income tax on profits earned from the business. A sole proprietorship is the simplest business to set up or take apart making it the most popular type to start.

Limited Liability Company (LLC) - This structure separates the business from the individual(s). The members of the company cannot be held personally responsible for the company's debts or liabilities. LLC's are essentially hybrid entities that combine the characteristics of a corporation and a partnership or sole proprietorship.

Partnership - A partnership happens when two or more individuals get together and agree to share the businesses profits and losses.

Corporation - This is an independent set up of a business. Separate from the individual(s) who created it, but often referred to as a "legal person". Like a person, the corporation can be taxed and can be held legally liable for its actions. The corporation can also make a profit. The key benefit of corporate status is the avoidance of personal liability. The primary disadvantage is the cost to form a corporation and the extensive record-keeping that's required.

Non-Profit Organization - Organized for the purpose other than generating profit, this type of business structure is granted the "tax-exempt" status by the Internal Revenue Service (IRS). These businesses pay no income tax on any money they earn through fundraising activities or the donations they receive.

Keep in mind that the business structure you start out with may not meet your needs in years to come. Many sole proprietorships evolve into some other form of business like a partnership or corporation as the company grows and the needs of the owners change.

The bottom line! Don't take this very important decision lightly, and don't make a choice based on what someone else has done. Carefully consider the unique needs of your business and its owners, and seek expert advice if needed, before settling on a particular business format.

Chapter 2
Getting Your Paperwork In Order

Getting your paperwork together is a very critical process when starting your business. Claiming a name is one thing but actually owning it is something different. After you choose your business structure and decide on a name, it's time to file your business formation paperwork. Our checklist provides you with the basic steps you should follow to start a business. Depending on your business, your state may have you take additional steps for your specific business type. Now let's make your business official! This is where we separate the realists from the hobbyists.

Now that you have decided on what type of business structure you are going to have lets make it official. The next step is apply for an EIN number. An Employer Identification Number (EIN) is also known as a Federal Tax Identification Number, and is used to identify a business entity. Many sole proprietorship business structures will allow you to use your social security number instead of an EIN. Knowing when to use either or is key. Heres how you can tell if you should request an EIN.

According to the IRS, your business must have an EIN if any of these criteria apply:

1. You have employees;
2. Your business operates as a corporation or a partnership;
3. You withhold taxes on income other than wages paid to a nonresident alien;
4. You have a tax-deferred pension plan; or
5. You're involved with certain organizations listed on the IRS website.

Outside of filing taxes, you may also need an EIN to:

1. Open a bank account in the name of your business;

2. Apply for a line of credit in the name of your business;
3. Apply for business permits; or
4. Furnish independent contractors

If you visit the IRS website they can provide you with an EIN number and letter online for your business immediately. You do not have to spend thousands of dollars on a lawyer or company to create your business for you when you can file the majority, if not all, of your paperwork online for less than $150 in most states.

Now its time to get your business license and register your name with the state. The best thing you will learn about starting a business is that it is a straight forward process. Since regulations may vary state-to-state its imperative that you visit your states website to understand the licensing requirements. To get a business license you can either download the required forms and application from your City's website or go to your local City Hall and pick them up in person. You should be prepared with the following information to complete the paperwork.

1. Your type of business
2. Business name
3. Business address
4. Name of business owner
5. Contact information
6. EIN number

Each city is different with its own requirements regarding filing fees for your business license, but once paid you officially are a business owner. Congrats on the big step and taking the risk taker leap of faith!

Most entrepreneurs grasp the importance of creating a great or catchy business name for branding. During this process new business owners spend many hours and days trying to brainstorm the perfect name. But after you have chosen the perfect name for your business, what's the next step to making sure everything is legal? Well that brings us to the final step in getting your paperwork in order and thats registering your name with the state your business operates in.

The key reason to register a business name is to prevent anyone else from using it. There have been so many cases where an individual will create a name for a company, brand and market the name, all for someone to come along and take it because the necessary paperwork wasn't filed. That person won't be you.

Here's what you need to do.

    1. First you need to check and make sure that your business name has not already been registered. Every state has a directory and most can be easily accessed online via the Secretary of State website.

    2. Second, start following the process explained on the website if your name is available to use. If you find out that your name is already taken, go back to the drawing board

and tweak your name a little bit more to make it more unique.

In most situations, if your business has been registered as a corporation, limited partnership, or LLC, the process will automatically register your business name with the state.

Now that you have ensured that the legal name of your business cannot be taken by anyone else in your state; let's try to see how we can finance the company. Great job!

Chapter 3
How To Finance Your Business

Finding financing in any economic condition can be challenging. Don't feel pressured to have a brick and mortar for your business because you see other entrepreneurs with one. However, if it is needed you need to prepare accordingly. Businesses spend money before they even open their doors; so where do you begin. Ask yourself the following questions. "How much money do I need to have upfront to start my business?" "What type of money do I need to have before I begin to see a profit?" This is an area that you must be very realistic about and research is essential. Having an unrealistic perception of your start up costs can be the beginning of the end, so pay close attention during this process.

Here are some of the most important things that you need to take into account when factoring in your startup costs for financing your business.

1. List the equipment, furniture, supplies and how many people are needed to operate your business.

2. Itemize startup costs for inventory, signage, sales and marketing literature, permits, operating capital, and legal or professional fees.

3. Tally up your monthly overhead for rent, utilities, business insurance and taxes.

4. Factor in your employee or contractor wages.

A good rule of thumb is to assume everything will cost more than you expect. As you tally up everything, always add a little more to your numbers to create a safety net. Your financial situation is an obvious factor that determines the type of business you can afford. However, if you have no money or bad credit don't let that discourage you. It can still work but often times is much harder. Yes, there will be ridiculously long days with little to no sleep. Yes, you are going to be stressed. But those that want it bad enough will make it. So now that we know what you are going to need money for to start your business let's try to find out the options available to you to get things going.

In today's society you have to be creative and think outside of the box when it comes to financing your business. Loans are accessible for those who qualify but they are highly competitive. Most entrepreneurs piece together their financing from several different sources. You have to make the best decision for your business based on your current need.

Let's go over the most common and relatively accessible ways to get financing for your business. Please remember that where and how you finance your business can be the difference between success and failure.

- **Factoring** - Factoring is a finance method where a company sells its receivables at a discount to get cash up-front. It's often used by companies with poor credit or by businesses such as apparel manufacturers, which have to fill orders long before they get paid.

• **Bank loans & Line of Credit** - Lending standards have gotten much stricter, but there are quite a few banks that have earmarked additional funds for small business lending.

• **Crowdfunding** - A crowdfunding site like gofundme.com or kickstarter.com can be fun and effective in trying to raise money for your business.

• **Family & Friends** - Turning to your family and friends is the most common way to finance a start-up. However, beware when you turn loved ones into creditors, you're risking their financial future and jeopardizing important personal relationships.

• **Microloans** - Microloans are often so small that commercial banks can't be bothered lending the funds. Instead of a bank, you need to turn to a microlender such as a non-profit organization that works differently than banks.

Microlenders offer smaller loan sizes, usually require less documentation than banks, and often apply more flexible underwriting criteria. You can also search these kind of providers under local and state economic development organizations.

• **Angel investors** - Angel investors are private individuals or small groups of executives who invest in businesses, usually by making an equity purchase. They can provide money, expertise, and guidance to help start and grow a business.

• **Grants** - Businesses focused on science or research may be able to get grants from the Small Business Administration (SBA). The SBA offers grants through the Small Business Innovation Research (SBIR) and Small Business Technology Transfer (STTR) programs.

• **Your Assets** - The majority of your start up financing comes directly from your own pocket. Even if you don't have a lot of money in your checking or savings accounts there are other ways to leverage your assets such as selling your high end items that you don't need or use.

- **Venture Capital**- Pursuing venture capital means bringing someone else, generally a stranger, into your business as a partial owner. Usually, you will not receive any profit yourself until your investor owner has profited from your business.

When it comes to financing your business there isn't any one-size-fits-all method that can easily be applied in choosing what option works best for you. Remember each business has its own unique requirements. So it makes sense to try a few different routes to obtain financing.

Now that you have transitioned your idea to reality, made it legal and have the financing to make a huge impact on the economy. Congratulations risk taker! It's time to grow your business.

Chapter 4
Marketing & Branding Your Business

Branding: Who you are

Marketing: How you build awareness about who you are

Marketing and branding go hand in hand. This is an area where a lot of small businesses fail to recognize its importance. Marketing starts at the very beginning! If your wondering why, it's because you have to gage your target market to see if your idea has the potential to be a viable business. As a small business you must do everything within your means to promote your product and/or service. It's just as important to market a small business as it is to market a major corporation.

Building your brand is the other crucial part of developing your business. You need branding because it increases your value, provides your employees with direction and motivation, and it also makes it easier to attract new customers. In order to succeed in branding, you must understand the needs and wants of your customers. Think of branding as the expression of who you are as a business and what you offer.

Contrary to belief there are some pretty creative ways to market and brand your business without a lot of money. Although it may require a huge investment of your time, the return you get on it will not go unnoticed. A lot of times it can actually help you save money in the long run as you continue to grow your business. The goal is to spend less and make more.

Here are some of the most common and cost effective ways to market your business:

• **Social Media** - It's free and easy to get started and offers a massive network of potential customers.

- **Contests and Giveaways** - Everyone loves free gifts! Give away desirable or fun items to build brand awareness and connect your brand with customers.

- **Team up with your Partners** - To help keep costs low it makes sense to partner with other complementary businesses.

- **Email Marketing** - Not only is email marketing a low-cost method for getting the word out but it also offers one of the best returns on the investment of your time.

- **Referral Marketing** - This is word-of-mouth advertising and by far one of the most effective and low-cost ways to market your business. Ask your customers for leads and make sure you follow up.

- **Blogging** - A blog not only helps your business get its name out through followers, but it is a way to connect with your consumers more directly.

- **Network** - Attend networking events. The saying goes "It's not what you know, but who you know."

- **Design a Website** - Your website must attract attention and give value to those who visit. Use it as a tool to retain and keep in touch with existing customers as well as for enticing new customers.

- **Marketing Materials**: This includes your business card, brochures, sales letters, signage and car decals. These speak volumes about your business.

If you are not marketing your business, you are not making progress. No matter how great you may think your product or service is, without any marketing efforts, you are more likely at a stand still. Marketing isn't rocket science, but it isn't necessarily straightforward either. So to get your business off to the right start, make it your business to let people know that your business exists.

Now flipping to the other hand. Remember, there is a true link between successful businesses and strong branding. Here are some of the most effective ways to aid you in the brand process:

- Determine your brand's target audience.

- Define a branding mission statement.

- Research brands within your industry niche.

- Outline the key qualities & benefits your brand offers.

- Create a great brand logo & tagline.

- Form your brand's business voice.

- Build a brand message and elevator pitch.

- Integrate your brand into every aspect of your business.

- Always stay true to your brand.

Simply put, your brand is your promise to your customer. It tells them what they can expect from your products and services, and it also separates what you are offering from your competitors. Your brand is taken from who you are, who you want to be and who people recognize you as. Do your research and learn the needs of your customers. Do not rely on what you think they think. Its always best to know what they think.

Be mindful that starting and maintaining a business takes patience, dedication, passion and most importantly time! Now that you have marketed and branded your new business lets pull it all together and test the market. As an entrepreneurial risk taker, this is the fun part!

Chapter 5
Testing The Market

Being an entrepreneur is a role that's generally defined by long hours and large monetary risks. The world is competitive, and to make it anywhere requires perseverance. The bottom line is that you just have to get started. Luckily there are no limitations to entrepreneurship. You don't have to pass a test and you don't need to have tons of money.

Now that you have a new business, marketed and aligned your brand, its now time to introduce your product or service. Leaving out this step is like jumping off a plane into the ocean, blindfolded. Your time and money are extremely valuable to you as an entrepreneur so you can't afford to board that plane blindfolded. The more you test your product or service the better you will be able to produce and sell it. Always remember that every dollar you spend on testing the market will save you twice as many dollars in losses later on during your marketing process.

When you test the market you are simply just conducting an experiment comprised of real life buying situations. This is because it allows you to get an authentic reaction from your consumer. Now lets take your product and/or service and test the market. Here's how to begin:

Develop a layout of your product and/or service that you can show to others. A lot of times ideas for new products or services don't work the first time. When you develop a layout, you actually are able to create a visual to show. It also allows you to try it out for yourself to make sure it works.

Determine the price you can sell your product and/or service for in todays market. Call around to different places to get current pricing from suppliers. Try to figure out all the costs associated with bringing your product and/or service to market. Take into consideration the costs of equipment, shipping, loss, insurance, transportation, etc.

Go to a potential customer with your sample or layout and ask if they would buy it. Do a little survey to find out things like how much they would pay for your product and/or service. If you come across some people that criticize your new idea, make sure you ask them why and what would they suggest you change.

Compare your product and/or service with others that are currently out. Always ask yourself, "Why would someone switch and buy from me?"

Ultimately, the real test becomes taking your new product and/or service to a customer who can buy it and determine if they like it. Your ability to sell will be one of the biggest and most important skills that you will acquire. It will be advantageous to your brand to listen and take all of the comments and objections of your buyers into consideration. Their feedback is priceless.

Continually tweaking your ideas over and over as opposed to sticking with your original idea will help ensure your products success. Don't be afraid to be different or think outside of the box. Remember if no one knows you have a product and/or service that's just like not having a product and/or service. There will be times that you will stumble or lose focus but during those times ask yourself one simple question. Why did I decide to be an Entrepreneur aka Risk Taker?

Well this is the end, I hope you have found this book to be helpful, motivational and foundation building. Remember to always stay consistent, passionate and hungry!

Notes

Notes

www.ingramcontent.com/pod-product-compliance
Lightning Source LLC
Chambersburg PA
CBHW050036230526
45470CB00003B/1312